EYEWITNESS DISASTER

EARTHQUAKES!

HELEN DWYER

Marshall Cavendish
Benchmark
New York

This edition first published in 2011 in the United States of America
by MARSHALL CAVENDISH BENCHMARK
An imprint of Marshall Cavendish Corporation

Other Marshall Cavendish Offices:
Marshall Cavendish International (Asia) Private Limited, 1 New Industrial Road, Singapore 536196 • Marshall Cavendish International (Thailand) Co Ltd. 253 Asoke, 12th Flr, Sukhumvit 21 Road, Klongtoey Nua, Wattana, Bangkok 10110, Thailand • Marshall Cavendish (Malaysia) Sdn Bhd, Times Subang, Lot 46, Subang Hi-Tech Industrial Park, Batu Tiga, 40000 Shah Alam, Selangor Darul Ehsan, Malaysia

Marshall Cavendish is a trademark of Times Publishing Limited

Planned and produced by Discovery Books Ltd., 2 College Street, Ludlow, Shropshire, SY8 1AN www.discoverybooks.net
Managing editor: Rachel Tisdale
Editor: Helen Dwyer
Designer: sprout.uk.com Limited
Illustrators: Keith Williams, sprout.uk.com Limited, (pages 4, 8 and 9), Stefan Chabluk (page 10)
Picture researcher: Rachel Tisdale

Photo acknowledgments: Corbis: 11 (Zhou Chao/epa), 14 (Bettmann), 16 (Craig Aurness), 18 (Roger Ressmeyer), 19 (Jim Sugar), 25 (Jeremy Horner), 27 (Reuters/Simon Kwong), 29 (China Daily/Reuters). FEMA: 24 (Casey Deshong). Getty Images: cover (Koichi Kamoshida), 5 (Joe Raedie/Staff), 6 (Adek Berry/AFP), 7 (Sankei Archive), 12 (Warrick Page), 13 (Paula Bronstein), 15 (Ernesto Benavides/AFP), 20 (Sankei Archive), 21 (Johnson Liu/AFP), 22 (Vincenzo Pinto/AFP), 23 (Franco Origlia). Istockphoto.com: 28 (Guillermo Montesinos). Wikimedia: 17 (H D Chadwick).
Cover Picture: Rescue workers at work in Nagaoka, Japan, following a series of powerful earthquakes that rocked northern Japan.

Library of Congress Cataloging-in-Publication Data

Dwyer, Helen.
  Earthquakes / by Helen Dwyer.
    p. cm. -- (Eyewitness disaster)
  Includes bibliographical references and index.
  ISBN 978-1-60870-001-1
  1. Earthquakes--Juvenile literature. I. Title.
  QE521.3.D892 2010
  551.22--dc22
                                2009042151

Printed in China

CONTENTS

Words in **bold** or <u>underlined</u> are defined
in the Glossary on page 30.

WHAT IS AN EARTHQUAKE?

Earthquakes take place all the time. Every year, half a million quakes shake our planet's surface. But only about a fifth of these quakes are felt by us humans—the rest can only be detected by scientific equipment.

An earthquake is a movement in the ground. It is caused by events taking place inside Earth's solid upper layer. This layer consists of the **crust** and the top part of the **mantle** that lies below it. This solid layer is broken up into several large sections, called **tectonic plates**, which move around very, very slowly above the hotter, more liquid part of the mantle.

> "In a moment I was [woken by] a most horrid crash.... The house I was in shook with such violence, that the upper stories immediately fell ... the walls continued rocking to and fro ... opening in several places; large stones falling down on every side from the cracks."
>
> *Charles Davy, survivor of the Lisbon earthquake, 1755.*

Colliding Tectonic Plates

Tectonic plates travel in different directions. As they move past, under, or over each other, their edges can become stuck together. Eventually the pressure exerted by the moving plates is so great that they break free. The energy that is released moves away in all directions like waves or ripples on a pond. These ripples are called **seismic waves**. They cause the shaking and moving of the ground that people call an earthquake.

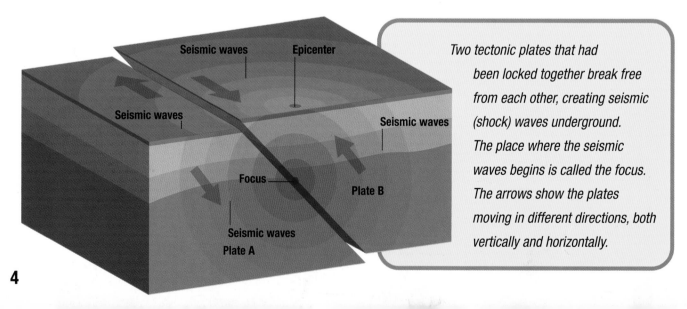

Seismic waves Epicenter

Seismic waves

Seismic waves

Focus

Plate B

Seismic waves
Plate A

Two tectonic plates that had been locked together break free from each other, creating seismic (shock) waves underground. The place where the seismic waves begins is called the focus. The arrows show the plates moving in different directions, both vertically and horizontally.

Focus and Epicenter

An earthquake begins in the rocks below the surface of Earth. The place where it begins is known as the **focus**. The depth of the focus differs with every earthquake—from just below the surface to nearly 435 miles (700 kilometers) deep. The point on the surface directly above the focus is called the **epicenter**.

A Series of Earthquakes

A powerful earthquake may be followed by weaker **aftershocks** as Earth's crust adjusts after the main quake. In contrast, a series of small earthquakes may occur before a bigger one.

In January 2010 an earthquake on the Caribbean island of Haiti destroyed countless buildings and killed thousands of people in and around the capital, Port-au-Prince.

EARTHQUAKE STORIES

Before people knew what caused earthquakes they tried to explain them in stories. Many of these tales involve animals. In Siberia (northeastern Asia), people thought that Earth rested on a sled pulled by dogs that were infested with fleas. Whenever a dog stopped to scratch itself, Earth shook. In other stories, animals held up Earth: in Japan it was a catfish; in India it was either elephants or snakes; and in Mongolia it was a giant, twitching frog. When the animal moved, Earth shook. Native peoples in California thought that Earth was being pulled apart by huge turtles.

THE DANGERS OF EARTHQUAKES

Earthquakes rank with floods, famines and tropical storms as the most dangerous of natural disasters. In the twenty-first century, almost half a million people have died as a result of earthquakes.

An earthquake is most dangerous and destructive if it occurs near Earth's surface. Places closest to the epicenter suffer the most damage. The damage also depends on how easily the seismic waves move through the rocks and land features.

Extra Dangers

Earthquakes can trigger other dangerous natural events. The ground may break apart, leaving gaps several yards wide. When this happens, large structures such as bridges and dams may be destroyed.

The shaking can even change the soil, making it flow like a liquid for a short while. When this happens, buildings may sink into the soil or tip over. In hilly areas, quakes can trigger **landslides**, which can wipe out whole villages and towns.

Deadly Waves

Earthquakes in the seabed can trigger shock waves in the water, called **tsunamis**, which are very dangerous. Tsunamis travel at great speeds for hundreds or thousands of miles across oceans and can cause massive destruction in coastal areas.

In Pariaman, Indonesia, the earthquake in October 2009 caused many landslides. Here only a narrow band of houses remains standing between two landslides.

THE DESTRUCTION OF YUNGAY

In 1970 an undersea earthquake off the coast of Peru, in South America, brought disaster to the Andes mountains. The shaking dislodged a mountain **glacier**, which carried rocks, mud, snow, and ice down the mountainside. This landslide struck the town of Yungay three minutes later. Most of the 25,000 townspeople were buried or crushed. Only 350 people survived, most of them children at a circus. They were saved by a clown, who led them up a hill to safety.

"I could see a giant wave of gray mud about 60 meters [197 ft] high.... The sky went dark because of all the dust, mostly from all the destroyed homes."

Mateo Casaverde, survivor of the Yungay landslide, 1970.

Collapsing Structures

In many earthquakes, most injuries are caused by the failure of man-made structures. Poorly designed or flimsy buildings may collapse. Electrical power lines and gas and water pipes may break. As a result, people are left without shelter, power, and clean water. Gas that leaks out of broken pipes is especially dangerous because it can **ignite** and cause fires. If water supplies are also cut there may be no water to fight these fires.

Fires raged out of control, the day after an earthquake struck Kobe, Japan, in 1995. Gas leaks started many of the fires, and older wooden houses burned quickly.

EARTHQUAKE ZONES

Nearly all earthquakes occur in places close to where tectonic plates meet each other. People in those areas have to be aware that an earthquake could strike at any time.

Tectonic plates can collide in a variety of ways, but all these collisions cause earthquakes. There are two types of plates: oceanic (under the ocean) and continental (under the land). Oceanic plates are **denser** than continental plates.

Sinking Plates

Sometimes an oceanic plate is **subducted** (sinks) under a continental plate or under another oceanic plate. For example, the massive Pacific Plate is slowly moving northwestward. As it moves it sinks under the North American Plate.

Collisions on Land

When continental plates collide, both are of similar weight, so the rocks along the boundary are forced upward and form mountains. Sometimes—as along the San Andreas **Fault** in California—two plates slide horizontally past each other in different directions or at different speeds.

This world map shows the main tectonic plates. The arrows show the direction of movement.

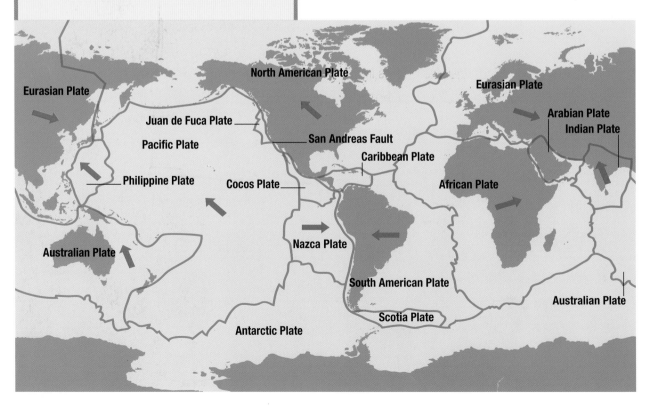

"We [felt] an earthquake, accompanied by a very awful noise [like] distant thunder.... The screams of the affrighted inhabitants running to and fro ... the cries of the fowls and beasts of every species, the cracking of trees falling ... formed a scene truly horrible."

Eliza Bryan, survivor of the 1811–1812 earthquakes in New Madrid, Missouri.

Far from the Edges

Occasionally, earthquakes occur in weak areas of Earth's crust far from tectonic plate edges. In 1811 and 1812 four major earthquakes—later known as the New Madrid earthquakes—took place in Arkansas and Missouri.

Every few years a minor quake strikes in Britain. In April 2007 the county of Kent was hit by a small earthquake, which damaged hundreds of buildings and was felt across the English Channel in France.

*An oceanic tectonic plate slides under a continental plate. The arrows show the direction of movement. As the plate sinks, earthquakes occur and the surface of the continental plate is pushed up to form mountains. The sinking plate eventually melts, creating **magma**, which may erupt as a volcano.*

AMAZING ESCAPE

Buried Alive—Twice

In 1976 an earthquake in Tangshan, China, killed 240,000 people. One miner, Alatanbagen Taoqi, was buried under **rubble** for ten days before he was rescued. Thirty-two years later an earthquake struck the Sichuan area and 60-year-old Taoqi was buried again, this time in an office building. A few hours later rescuers dug him out, still alive. He was the only survivor in the whole building.

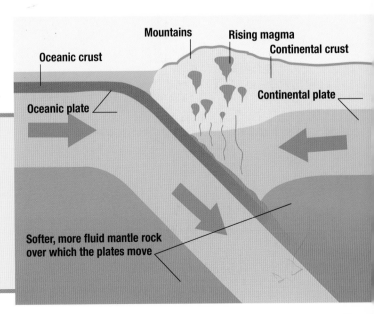

Mountains — Rising magma — Continental crust — Oceanic crust — Oceanic plate — Continental plate — Softer, more fluid mantle rock over which the plates move

CONTINENTS COLLIDE

Between 40 and 50 million years ago the Indian Plate collided with the Eurasian Plate. It was the climax of a journey that began about 150 million years before, when India was an island off the coast of Australia, thousands of miles from Asia.

Creating the Himalayas

About 200 million years ago the Indian Plate began to move about 3.5 inches (9 centimeters) north every year. When it struck the Eurasian continent, the rocks at the edges of both tectonic plates were pushed upward. These rocks very slowly formed the Himalaya mountains, which stretch for nearly 1,550 miles (2,500 km) along the border between India, Nepal, and China. Some of the mountains, including Everest, are now more than 5.5 miles (9 km) high.

India continues to move northward, pressing further into Asia. As a result the Himalayas are still rising by about 0.4 inch (1 cm) every year and the mountainous region of Tibet, in China, is pushing parts of Asia east.

Stresses and Quakes

These movements of the Indian Plate cause massive earthquakes every few years in the region. In the twenty-first century there have already been disastrous earthquakes in Pakistan, India, Central Asia, and China. In May 2008 an earthquake in Sichuan, China, killed about 90,000 people and left five million homeless.

Epicenters of major earthquakes since 2000

Boundary of tectonic plates

KAZAKHSTAN

MONGOLIA

UZBEKISTAN
KYRGYZSTAN
TAJIKISTAN
TURKMENISTAN
2002
2002
2001
2005
AFGHANISTAN
Tibet
2008
2008
Sichuan
PAKISTAN
NEPAL
BHUTAN
CHINA
2001
BANGLADESH
INDIA
MYANMAR LAOS VIETNAM
Indian
Ocean
Bay
of
Bengal
THAILAND
N
CAMBODIA
W E
S
1,000 miles
1,000 kilometers

The collision between India and the rest of Eurasia not only created the vast Himalaya mountain range, but also causes frequent earthquakes. Recent quakes are marked on the map. They show that even areas far away from the plate boundary are affected.

A soldier carries an elderly man on his back in the panic to get out of a town in Sichuan, China, in 2008. People feared that a flood of water upriver would burst through the dam of debris, or rubble, left by the earthquake.

RACE AGAINST TIME

The 2008 Sichuan earthquake triggered landslides that dammed many rivers, creating new lakes. Scientists realized that one new dam on the Jianjiang River would soon burst and send a 66-foot-high (20-m) wall of rocks, soil, and water down the valley toward the large city of Mianyang. Something had to be done quickly.

A decision was made to release the water in a different direction. Explosives were used to create a new channel from the lake through the town of Beichuan, which had already been evacuated after earthquake damage. Although the people of Beichuan had to move into new homes, more than a million people downstream in Mianyang were saved from a disastrous flood and landslide.

A soldier carries an elderly man on his back in the panic to get out of a town in Sichuan, China, in 2008. People feared that a flood of water upriver would burst through the dam of debris, or rubble, left by the earthquake.

" These dams are ... weak, loose piles of debris, under huge pressure from the river water building up behind. One more aftershock could suddenly transform this.... It would rush off downstream, bulldozing and burying everything in its path."

Geologist Stephen Edwards.

"Each village has about 250 houses. All of them are destroyed."

KASHMIR OCTOBER 8, 2005

Reporters and aid workers who rushed to the earthquake zone described the situation to people across the world:

> "Almost every shop in the bazaar is destroyed, the goods . . . now strewn across the twisted mass of wreckage. Mosques are down . . . along with . . . hundreds of homes and also schools."
> Andrew North, reporter in Balakot

"The road has been blocked by a landslide . . . beyond . . . are many villages. People have come from these small mountain villages carrying the injured on their shoulders, walking for hours. Each village has about 250 houses. All of them are destroyed."
Dr. Irfan Noor, Mansehra district

The region of Kashmir is on the border between India and Pakistan. It also sits on the boundary between the Indian and Eurasian Plates. On October 8, 2005, a major earthquake occurred in Kashmir. About 75,000 people died as buildings collapsed on them. These victims included 18,000 children who were attending schools and colleges when the earthquake struck.

An apartment building in Islamabad, the capital of Pakistan, was completely destroyed by the earthquake.

A homeless family cooks lentils over a fire in Balakot, Pakistan, where 90 percent of the houses were destroyed. Many of the homeless had to endure a winter living in tents.

Destruction in the Mountains

Most of the damage was in remote mountain areas, where whole villages of mud-brick houses were destroyed. Help was slow in reaching survivors because landslides had blocked or destroyed many roads. More than a thousand aftershocks over the next three weeks also created difficulties for rescue teams.

A Race Against Time

Yet another problem was that winter was beginning in Kashmir. Snow began to fall five days after the quake. It became a race against time to get homeless survivors to safety. Helicopters were used to fly in food, medicine, tents, and blankets and to take out injured people and children who had lost their parents.

Helping Hands

The Pakistani government asked the North Atlantic Treaty Organization (NATO) for aid. NATO is a military **alliance** that was set up after World War II to defend its member countries in North America and western Europe from attack. It now includes Turkey and countries in eastern Europe.

NATO helicopters flew to mountain villages, delivering supplies and taking out the injured. NATO's engineers built shelters and repaired the damaged roads. Medical teams opened a temporary hospital to perform operations and set up medical units that could be moved from place to place.

ALONG THE EASTERN PACIFIC

Many powerful earthquakes occur along the western coasts of North and South America as oceanic tectonic plates sink under continental plates.

Alaskan Earthquakes

Along the coast of Alaska the Pacific Plate is subducting under the North American Plate. One of the biggest earthquakes ever recorded took place in Alaska in 1964. In some regions the shaking changed the structure of the soil so that it flowed like liquid. Buildings sank into the soil or tipped over. In other areas, landslides caused much of the damage.

The massive 1964 earthquake caused chaos in Anchorage, Alaska. Here sections of a road have collapsed and fallen about 20 feet (6 m).

THE JUAN DE FUCA PLATE

The Juan de Fuca Plate is a small tectonic plate that sinks under the coast of North America. It has created the Cascade Range of volcanic mountains which stretch for 620 miles (1,000 km) from Vancouver Island in Canada to northern California. Scientists fear that a big earthquake may occur here in the next fifty years, threatening the cities of Vancouver, Seattle, Portland, and Victoria. In the meantime though, scientists are studying a series of hundreds of earthquakes that took place deep in the ocean floor in the middle of the Juan de Fuca Plate in 2008. **Marine** geologist Robert Dziak said: "The fact that it's taking place in the middle of the plate . . . is puzzling. It's something worth keeping an eye on."

Mexican Earthquakes

Off the west coast of Central America, the oceanic Cocos Plate sinks under the lighter Caribbean Plate, creating an earthquake zone extending north into Mexico. In 1985 a disastrous quake off the Mexican coast killed thousands of people in Mexico City.

South American Earthquakes

Almost the entire west coast of South America lies on the boundaries of the Nazca Plate and the South American Plate. The oceanic Nazca Plate moves eastward by nearly 1.5 inches (3.7 cm) every year. As it sinks under the continent it sets off earthquakes. The most recent major quake was in 2007 under the ocean near Peru.

"Everything was trembling—cars, the floor, walls—and there were odd lights that illuminated the sky many times. People were screaming and hugging because it was so long."

"I have experienced tremors before, but never standing out in the street watching the trees swaying, light posts bending, and actually feeling the waves under my feet, with my knees shaking."

Eyewitnesses to the 2007 earthquake in Peru.

The earthquake in Peru in 2007 disrupted water supplies in the town of Pisco. The local people had to collect drinking water from a tank truck.

THE SAN ANDREAS FAULT

Inland from the coast of California, the Pacific and North American plates meet. The Pacific Plate is moving northwest, while the North American Plate moves southeast. This boundary forms a 9-mile-deep (15-km), 810-mile-long (1,300-km) **fracture** in the rocks, known as the San Andreas Fault.

A Constant Threat

As the two plates push past each other, movements along the fault are usually slow and steady, causing minor but frequent earthquakes. However, parts of the plates sometimes become stuck for many years, so pressure builds up. When the plates break free from one another, this pressure is released and big quakes occur.

San Francisco, 1906

In 1906 a large earthquake occurred on the San Andreas Fault. The city of San Francisco was badly hit and many buildings collapsed. The quake was followed by fires, which were caused by gas pipes and chimneys breaking, stoves overturning, and electric cables touching each other. Four days later, when the fires were finally put out, 80 percent of San Francisco had been destroyed, more than 3,000 people were dead, and a quarter of a million people were homeless.

The spectacular San Andreas Fault is easy to see from the air. For millions of years two tectonic plates have slid past each other in opposite directions, creating mountain ranges and triggering earthquakes.

RAGING FIRES

In San Francisco in 1906, fires caused more destruction than the earthquake. The city's fire department had no water to fight the fires because water mains and the supply pipes from reservoirs had been broken. Some houses were blown up with dynamite to create gaps so the fire could not spread. Unfortunately the explosions created even more fires. Then a navy officer arrived and ordered all the tugboats in the harbor to pump seawater out of the bay and feed it into the firefighters' hoses. At last the fire department was able to control the fires.

An area of San Francisco that was badly damaged in the 1906 earthquake and fire. Very few buildings were undamaged and many were simply rubble.

" Power and trolley lines snapped like threads. The ends of the power lines dropped to the pavement ... writhing and hissing like reptiles. Brick and glass showered about me.... Buildings crumbled like card houses ... a second shock hit ... I was thrown flat and the cobblestones danced like corn in a popper."

Thomas Jefferson Chase, survivor of the San Francisco earthquake and fire, 1906.

"It was moving like a wave, just like water."

SAN FRANCISCO, CALIFORNIA OCTOBER 17, 1989

Army Staff Sergeant David Langdon was at a baseball game in San Francisco when the earthquake occurred.

"The spooky part . . . was looking up in the stands, completely full. . . . To see the slabs above the upper deck separate by feet and come back together, and watch the light stanchions [upright posts] sway left and right . . . about fifteen feet either way, it was a sight to behold. . . . Then to look out to the field and just see it roll as if it were an ocean, because it was moving like a wave, just like water; waves and waves and waves."

On October 17, 1989, a part of the San Andreas Fault that had been stuck since the 1906 earthquake suddenly moved. The earthquake that followed lasted 15 seconds and caused severe damage in the San Francisco Bay area.

Empty Roads

The quake struck at 5 p.m., just as a professional baseball game between two local teams, the Oakland Athletics and the San Francisco Giants, was starting in San Francisco. Fortunately, many people

This building in San Francisco sank into the soil because the earthquake changed the soil's structure and made it act like a liquid. The car is trapped underneath the third floor of the building.

The remains of the Cypress Freeway in West Oakland, where 42 people were killed when the top deck collapsed and crushed their cars.

had left work early or stayed in town to watch the game on TV, so the roads were much emptier than usual. If the traffic had been as heavy as it normally was at that time of day, many more people would have been killed or injured.

Death and Destruction

Most of the deaths and injuries occurred on a highway **viaduct** in West Oakland, where the top deck of the bridge collapsed onto the lower deck.

In Santa Cruz—near the earthquake's epicenter—many historic buildings collapsed and six people died. In San Francisco, multistory buildings in the Marina District were badly damaged and a section of the San Francisco–Oakland Bay Bridge collapsed.

LIQUID SOIL

In San Francisco the collapsed highway viaduct and the badly damaged Marina District were built on marshland. Both these areas were filled in with rubble, sand, and dirt to make the ground firmer before construction began. However, the shaking during an earthquake makes the wet, unstable soil behave like a liquid. Buildings on solid rock are much less likely to collapse during an earthquake.

EASTERN ASIA AND THE PACIFIC PLATE

Several countries in eastern Asia—especially Japan, Taiwan, and the Philippines—face the same problems as the western coasts of the Americas. They are located where continental and oceanic tectonic plates meet, so they are prone to frequent earthquakes.

The Kobe Earthquake

The islands that make up Japan were created by plate boundary movements. In 1995 a powerful quake struck the region of Kobe in southern Japan, where two million people live. Many old houses collapsed because their wooden walls were badly damaged and could no longer support their heavy tiled roofs. The tiles fell, crushing the floors below. In contrast, modern buildings, which were designed to withstand earthquakes, suffered minimal damage.

"Roof tiles clogged the street. Dust filled the air. Smoke was rising. The smell of gas filled the world."

Kurt Mundt, survivor of the earthquake in Kobe, Japan, 1995.

The force of the Kobe earthquake crumpled up this main road, which toppled on its side. Many roads and railways were badly damaged in the quake.

A block of flats in Wufeng, Taiwan, tilts dangerously after the earthquake in 1999, the most destructive earthquake on the island in more than sixty years. Since 1999, Taiwan has experienced several smaller earthquakes.

Taiwan Disaster

The island of Taiwan is another earthquake disaster area. Quakes in Taiwan usually begin under the sea, but in 1999 the island was devastated by a quake that originated under the island. Fifty thousand homes were destroyed and 2,400 people died. In many areas the quake triggered landslides which crushed houses under tons of rock. The damage was so serious because Taiwan's cities are not built on solid rock. The ground consists of rocks and rubble that have fallen or been washed down from the mountains.

AMAZING ESCAPE

Miracle Survivor

In 1990 an earthquake struck Baguio City in the Philippines. A 27-year-old physical fitness instructor named Pedrito Dy found himself trapped under rubble in the basement of a hotel that had collapsed. With no food to eat, Dy survived by dipping pieces of foam rubber into rainwater that fell through the rubble. He even drank his own urine. Finally, after fifteen days, rescuers spotted Dy's hand in the rubble and pulled him out, bruised but uninjured.

"I was hungry, thirsty and scared ... I lost hope several times ... I just waited for death to come.... It was a miracle."

Pedrito Dy, survivor of an earthquake in the Philippines, 1990.

"I was flung around like a rag doll."

L'AQUILA, ITALY APRIL 6, 2009

Shaken survivors told reporters how they escaped from damaged buildings in the middle of the night:

> "Everything fell, the plaster from the walls and all the furniture . . . the way to the stairs was blocked by a piece of furniture. . . . When we eventually got out to the street . . . another terrible shock occurred. We thought we could be hit by the collapsing rooftops, by bricks and plaster."
Vittorio Perfetto, in L'Aquila

"The walls shook violently and I was flung around like a rag doll . . . I was able to escape through a stairwell that was crumbling as I ran down it. The rest of the village looked like a battlefield and was mostly destroyed. It looked like a massive bomb had gone off."
Gabriel Kornel, in the village of San Gregorio near L'Aquila

Italy, in southern Europe, is part of a very active and complicated earthquake zone. In April 2009, the country experienced its worst quake in nearly thirty years.

Trapped in Bed

After two smaller earthquakes the day before, the main earthquake struck the city of L'Aquila and surrounding towns and villages in the middle of the night, when most people were in their homes in bed. Several buildings collapsed and thousands more were damaged. Rescue efforts to help people trapped by rubble were made more difficult by several minor aftershocks over the next few days. In all, more than 300 people died and 65,000 others saw their homes destroyed.

Italian fire-service workers carry an injured victim on a stretcher out of a damaged building.

INADEQUATE BUILDINGS

After the quake, many Italians demanded to know why modern buildings—even ones that were supposed to be earthquake-proof —had collapsed or been badly damaged. One of these buildings was a new hospital. As its walls gave way, medical staff had to get the patients out and then treat the injured outdoors.

Experts said later that building standards were not enforced properly in Italy. They believed that the new hospital was poorly built. It should have been able to withstand a severe earthquake.

Why Was the Damage So Bad?

The earthquake was very damaging for a number of reasons: the epicenter of the quake was very close to the surface—only 6 miles (10 km) underground; the city of L'Aquila was built on the unstable bed of an ancient lake which made the shaking stronger; and the city contained many buildings hundreds of years old that were not built to resist earthquakes.

L'Aquila is full of old, historic buildings. Many of them were destroyed or badly damaged.

UNDERSEA EARTHQUAKES AND TSUNAMIS

Tsunamis are giant ocean waves that are caused by the movements of earthquakes under the seafloor or by landslides that tumble into the sea. Tsunamis travel across oceans at speeds of up to 620 miles per hour (1,000 kph) and may be more than 50 feet (15 m) high when they reach land.

Long-distance Travelers

Not surprisingly, these waves can cause enormous damage when they reach a shore. Earthquakes along the western coasts of the Americas—from Alaska to Chile—have caused tsunamis that traveled across the Pacific as far as Hawaii and Japan.

Destruction in Portugal

In 1755 an earthquake in the Atlantic Ocean to the west of Portugal destroyed many buildings in Lisbon, Portugal's capital city. Forty minutes later a tsunami swept over the harbor, through the city and up the River Tagus. The giant waves caused death and destruction along the southern coast of Portugal.

A Pacific Ocean tsunami struck Samoa and American Samoa in the South Pacific in September 2009. This is the badly damaged village of Leone in American Samoa.

"The ground shook.... The buildings started to fall down. The only noise was tumbling <u>masonry</u> and the screams of [people] trapped in the church.... I could see the sea disappearing as if sucked down a hole. Then the ocean returned, all at once, taking with it the church ... and the bridge."

Report on the 1755 earthquake and tsunami from a priest in the Algarve region of Portugal.

The 2004 Indian Ocean Disaster

In 2004 a massive earthquake occurred under the Indian Ocean. It lasted for more than eight minutes and the movements in the seabed extended across 1,000 miles (1,600 km). The tsunamis that followed traveled as far as the coast of southern Africa. Altogether 230,000 people died in eleven countries around the Indian Ocean.

A tsunami wave created by an earthquake under the Indian Ocean hits a popular vacation spot in Thailand in the 2004 disaster.

TSUNAMI WARNING?

Japanese **seismologists** are eager to find out what is happening under the oceans around Japan so that they will have some warning before earthquakes or tsunamis strike. Scientists are now boring holes in the seafloor near Japan to collect rock samples. These samples can be analyzed to show where the worst stresses are. Japanese scientists plan to run an undersea cable to this region so that data from scientific instruments can be sent back to Japan. The information collected may help to predict the next big earthquake or tsunami.

MEASURING AND PREDICTING QUAKES

The strength, or **magnitude**, of an earthquake is usually expressed in the moment magnitude scale, which is very similar to the earlier Richter scale. It grades an earthquake in numbers from one to ten. In this system, a magnitude 6 earthquake is ten times bigger than one of magnitude 5, which is ten times bigger than a magnitude 4 quake.

The easiest way to understand these numbers is to have an idea of the damage the quakes cause. For example, an earthquake that measures between 4 and 5 will make objects inside a house shake, but it will not damage the house; one that measures between 8 and 9 can cause serious damage for hundreds of miles around the epicenter.

Seismographs

Earthquake vibrations are detected and recorded by electronic instruments called **seismographs**. The measurements can tell scientists how far away the earthquake began and how powerful it was. Measurements taken by several seismographs in different places indicate where the earthquake began.

Detecting Changes

Earthquake prediction is not very accurate, but scientists are constantly working to improve it. They measure gases and magnetic activity in Earth as well as stresses in rocks. They also study past earthquakes, looking for earthquake patterns that repeat themselves.

EARTHQUAKE STRENGTH

Magnitude	Description	Effects	Frequency
0–2.9	Micro	Usually not felt	Thousands every day
3.0–3.9	Minor	Often felt but rarely damaging	About 50,000 every year
4.0–4.9	Light	Objects in buildings shake or rattle	More than 6,000 every year
5.0–5.9	Moderate	Damage locally to poorly constructed buildings	About 800 every year
6.0–6.9	Strong	Slight damage to well-constructed buildings	About 120 every year
7.0–7.9	Major	Moderate damage to well-constructed buildings	About 18 every year
8.0–8.9	Great	Serious damage over hundreds of miles	About 1 every year
9.0–9.5	Great	Serious damage over thousands of miles	About 1 every 20 years

*A seismologist at Taiwan's Central Weather Bureau points out the differences between two earthquakes that occurred on the island on the same day in 2001. The computer printout of the vibrations is called a **seismogram**.*

SENSITIVE SNAKES

Scientists in China believe that snakes can be used to predict earthquakes because they behave strangely as early as five days before and as far as 75 miles (120 km) away. The Chinese now study the behavior of some captive snakes on video 24 hours a day, looking for signs that an earthquake is about to occur.

"Of all the creatures on the earth, snakes are perhaps the most sensitive to earthquakes. When an earthquake is about to occur, snakes will move out of their nests, even in winter ... the snakes will even smash into walls while trying to escape."

Jiang Weisong, Nanning, China, earthquake bureau director.

Scientists in Parkfield, California, think that sensitive new instruments may be able to detect tiny changes in the rocks a few hours before an earthquake. That would be long enough to get people away from buildings and to alert the emergency services.

Clues in Nature

Nature may also provide warnings of earthquakes. For centuries, sudden heat waves, brilliant lights in the sky, and changes in water levels in lakes, ponds and wells have all been felt and seen before earthquakes. Animals seem to register natural changes better than humans do. In Tangshan, China, in 1976, people noticed that several species of animals became agitated before a major earthquake.

PREPARING FOR EARTHQUAKES

In an earthquake, most deaths and injuries occur when buildings collapse. Even in minor earthquakes, buildings are damaged.

Building Design

Some older structures can withstand earthquakes quite well. Pyramid-shaped structures are very stable. Dry stone walls and timber-framed buildings can survive earthquakes because the separate parts can move slightly without the whole structure falling apart.

Architects now know a lot about designing buildings to resist earthquakes. Steel is used to strengthen concrete, stone, and **mortar**. Another way of stabilizing buildings is to build in special structures called **dampers**, which absorb the shaking. If an earthquake shakes the foundations, the vibration does not affect the rest of the building.

> "The world's exploding mega-cities have yet to experience a major earthquake, but it's only a matter of time before one or more occurs."
>
> *Roger Bilham, seismologist.*

Unstable Ground

Perhaps the most important safety measure of all is to avoid building on unstable ground in earthquake zones. Wet ground, sandy soil, clay, and rubble all transmit seismic waves very easily and even **amplify** them.

Torre Mayor in Mexico City is one of the most earthquake-resistant structures ever built. It is designed to withstand an earthquake with a magnitude of 8.5.

LESSONS FROM MEXICO CITY

In 1985 a Pacific Ocean earthquake caused the deaths of 10,000 people in Mexico City, 220 miles (350 km) away. Many buildings collapsed in the center of the city, which was built on an old lake bed with layers of sand, silt, and clay. This type of ground vibrates strongly when an earthquake strikes.

Between 1999 and 2003 a 55-story building called Torre Mayor was built on the old lake bed. Architects included lots of dampers in the design. These dampers absorb vibrations from quakes and prevent them from shaking the structure. When a strong earthquake occurred in Mexico City in 2003, the people in the building did not even feel it.

Safety Rules

However safe a building is, people still need to know how to act during an earthquake. The first thing to do is drop to the floor and cover yourself with something solid like a table. If this is not possible, sit against a wall away from windows and things that might fall on you.

If you are outdoors you must keep away from buildings, trees, and power lines because they could fall on you. After a quake there may be minor aftershocks—or even a stronger quake—so you must stay alert.

School children take part in an earthquake practice exercise at a school in China. This will help them know what to do if a real earthquake strikes.

GLOSSARY

aftershocks Smaller earthquakes that follow a large earthquake.

alliance A group, formed by a treaty, of countries that share the same interests.

amplify To make something stronger.

crust The outermost solid layer of Earth, between 3 and 30 miles (5 and 50 km) thick.

dampers Structures that absorb shocks and vibrations.

denser More solid; more tightly packed.

epicenter The point on Earth's surface directly above the place where an earthquake begins.

fault A large crack in Earth's crust where the rocks have moved in different directions.

focus The place where an earthquake begins.

fracture A crack in Earth's surface where stresses have made the rock break apart.

geologist A scientist who studies Earth's rocks.

glacier A slow-moving mass of ice that is formed from layers of crushed snow.

ignite To begin burning.

landslides Fast-moving masses of rocks and debris that travel quickly down a slope.

magma Liquid rock beneath the surface of Earth.

magnitude A measurement of the amount of energy released by an earthquake.

mantle The 1,900-mile-thick (3,000-km), mainly solid layer of Earth that is located directly beneath the crust.

marine Relating to the sea.

masonry Stonework.

mortar The mixture of cement, sand, and water that is placed between stones or bricks in buildings, to hold them together.

rubble Broken pieces of rocks resulting from the destruction of a building.

seismic wave The vibrations that travel through the ground during an earthquake.

seismogram A computer or paper record of an earthquake.

seismographs Instruments that detect and record the strength and direction of earthquakes.

seismologists Scientists who study earthquakes.

subducted When one tectonic plate is pushed under another.

tectonic plates The large sections of Earth's crust and upper mantle that move around independently, causing earthquakes.

tsunamis Waves caused by undersea earthquakes, volcanoes, or landslides.

viaduct An elevated roadway that enables vehicles to cross over a lower roadway.

FURTHER INFORMATION

Books

Farndon, John. *Predicting Earthquakes.* Why Science Matters. Chicago: Heinemann, 2009.

Fradin, Judy and Dennis. *Earthquakes.* Witness to Disaster. Des Moines, IA: National Geographic, 2008.

McLeish, Ewan. *Earthquakes in Action.* Natural Disasters in Action. New York: Rosen, 2009.

Woods, Michael and Mary B. *Earthquakes.* Disasters Up Close. Minneapolis, MN: Lerner, 2007.

Websites

www.earthquake.usgs.gov/learning/kids/
Earthquakes for Kids is a fun site by the U.S. Geological Survey. It features facts about earthquakes, photos, puzzles and games, earthquake history, project ideas, and much more!

www.fema.gov/kids/quake.htm
This site, run by the Federal Emergency Management Agency (FEMA), explains how earthquakes are measured, provides facts about earthquakes, and features some games. There is also a map that shows the areas of the United States that are most at risk from earthquakes.

www.nature.nps.gov/geology/usgsnps/pltec/
pltec1.html
This website provides an explanation of plate tectonics using diagrams of inside Earth and showing tectonic plate movements over time.

INDEX

Page numbers in **bold** are photographs or diagrams